It's All in the Family

Selected by Norma Vasey Webb
Illustrated by John Huehnergarth

It's All in the Family

Humorous Writings About the Pleasures and Perils of Family Life

HALLMARK EDITIONS

THE TWO OF US   5

KIDS!   22

ALL OF US   43

THE TWO OF US

GO AHEAD DEAR, I'M LISTENING

*The pitfalls of husband-wife conversations
receive the lighthearted scrutiny here of Corey
Ford. The selection is from his book,* Has
Anybody Seen Me Lately?:

When a husband is trying to peruse the sports
section of the Sunday newspaper while his wife
is reading aloud from the society column, it helps
to throw in certain key words from time to time,
to give the impression that he is paying attention. Veteran listeners are generally agreed that
the most popular of these is "Yes." To avoid
monotony, the simple affirmative may be rendered with various intonations, such as "Yaaah"
or "Yeh?" or "Mm hmh." Other breakfast sounds
that an engrossed husband may make are "Yunh"
(agreement), "Hgh!" (surprise), or "Hnph"
(sheer boredom). Sometimes it is sufficient just
to nod the head.

The danger in head-nodding is that the wife may switch without warning from Social Notes to Midsummer Sales, and the preoccupied husband will find himself committed to a promise before he realizes she has just said: "I see they've got a big reduction on drapes at Garfinkle's this week, don't you think it's time we did the living room over?" Just to be on the safe side, the breakfast listener would be prudent to alternate his nods between horizontal and vertical. I know one husband who has developed a slow roll of the head, transcribing a complete circle, which seems to have worked out very well. At least his living room hasn't been done over yet.

My own solution is a series of all-purpose answers which the husband may use whenever his wife starts telling him the strangest dream she had last night, or running over the household accounts, or reporting the latest bit of gossip she picked up at the bridge club yesterday. The objective is to keep the conversation going without becoming so involved that his mind will be distracted from the box scores. Let us say his wife is reading aloud a letter she has just received from her former roommate at Vassar, you remember Ethel Reebus, dear, the one with the braces on her teeth?

WIFE. Are you listening?

HUSBAND *engrossed in his paper*. Of course I'm listening, dear, I'm following every word.

WIFE. Ethel says they've had a lot of rain lately, her garden's coming fine, her husband sprained his back the other day.

HUSBAND *absently*. By the way, I hear he's quite an alcoholic.

This is good for at least seven uninterrupted minutes while his wife explains that he must be thinking of Ethel McAnkle, she's the one who lives in Denver, and anyway it wasn't her husband, it was her brother.

WIFE *continuing*. Ethel says they put in a new flagstone terrace in their patio.

HUSBAND. Isn't that (a) nice, (b) too bad, (c) just the kind of thing you might expect, though? *(Choice of one.)*

WIFE *suspiciously*. You're not paying any attention.

HUSBAND. Of course I am, dear, I'm just shading my eyes.

Wife continues reading while husband peruses paper. There is a sudden silence.

HUSBAND *quickly*. How much did it weigh?

This is based on the safe assumption that somewhere in any woman's letter somebody is bound to have just had a baby.

WIFE *excitedly*. Listen to this, they're planning

a trip East next spring.

HUSBAND *vaguely*. Who is?

WIFE. The Reebuses, of course.

HUSBAND *folding his paper and rising*. Say, speaking of Ethel Reebus, have you heard from her lately?

HUSBANDS ARE LIKE THAT

A husband works in subtle ways,
You really should behold one.
When wifey wants a dress or hat,
He says he loves the old one.

And when she speaks of dining out
As back when first he met her,
He says he doesn't mind, of course,
But likes her cooking better.

A husband is a cagey sort,
A smooth and clever article,
But I, for one, have yet to see
A wife who's fooled a particle.

RICHARD ARMOUR

Ne'er take a wife till thou hast a house (and a fire) to put her in.

BENJAMIN FRANKLIN

THE TROUBLE WITH WOMEN
IS MEN

A husband is a man who two minutes after his
head touches the pillow is snoring like an over-
loaded omnibus,

Particularly on those occasions when between the
humidity and the mosquitoes your own bed
is no longer a bed, but an insomnibus,

And if you turn on the light for a little reading
he is sensitive to the faintest gleam,

But if by any chance you are asleep and he wake-
ful, he is not slow to rouse you with the com-
plaint that he can't close his eyes, what about
slipping downstairs and freezing him a cooling
dish of pistachio ice cream.

His touch with a bottle opener is sure,

But he cannot help you get a tight dress over
your head without catching three hooks and
a button in your coiffure.

Nor can he so much as wash his ears without leaving an inch of water on the bathroom linoleum,

But if you mention it you evoke not a promise
to splash no more but a mood of deep melan-
cholium.

Indeed, each time he transgresses your chance of
correcting his faults grows lesser,

Because he produces either a maddeningly logical

explanation or a look of martyrdom which leaves you instead of him feeling the remorse of the transgressor.

Such are husbandly foibles, but there are moments when a foible ceases to be a foible.

Next time you ask for a glass of water and when he brings it you have a needle almost threaded and instead of setting it down he stands there holding it out to you, just kick him fairly hard in the stomach; you will find it thoroughly enjoible.

OGDEN NASH

THE FAMILY THAT TALKS THINGS OVER

Columnist Bill Vaughan's special kind of humor often focuses on family life. He discusses a 'typical' conversation between a wife and her husband in his book Bird Thou Never Wert:

She looked up from the magazine, regarded her husband silently for a moment, then inquired, "What was the best advice you ever had?"

"Shh!" he replied, gesturing toward the flickering television screen.

"But nothing's going on," she said; "just another cowboy falling down the stairs ". . .

"I know," he said with some exasperation, "but I like to hear it. Pow! as you say, and then buckety, bump, bump, buckety, phomp. I wouldn't give a plugged nickel for a Western show with a one-story saloon in it. I want to hear the dirty Black Hat tumbling down the steps and hitting every one of them. Well, you ruined it. Now what was it you asked me?"

"What was the best advice you ever had?" she repeated.

"Not to marry a gabby woman," he said. "Why?"

"Well," she said, "this magazine is paying money to people who write in and tell what was the best advice they ever had and how it affected their lives. So I thought if you could remember some good advice you had, why, you could write it up—Junior could help you with the spelling and Sue Jane could type it so the editors could read it —and get paid by this magazine."

"Never marry for anything but money," he said. "That was pretty good advice, and not taking it certainly had an effect on my life."

"I mean," she said impatiently, "some good advice you would want to pass on to your children."

"Never marry for anything but money."

"Cut it out," she said. "I mean seriously now."

"O.K.," he said. "This will take some thought."

For a few minutes there was no sound in the room except the voice of the announcer gently selling a patented aid for inner distress.

"That's funny," he said finally.

"What is?"

"All these people who can remember in print about the good advice they had. They don't seem to have any trouble dredging up some useful gem from the past, but I—"

"You can't think of anything?"

"Oh, no," he went on. "I can think of a lot of advice, darned good advice, that I have had over the years."

"Well, then—"

"The trouble is that I can't think of any that I was ever able to use. Like, 'Watch their eyes.' When I was a kid there was an old-timer in the neighborhood who claimed he had been a gun fighter in the West, and maybe he had. 'Always remember to watch their eyes, sonny,' he told me, many's the time. 'That's when you know they're about to make their play,' he said. 'Ninety-nine times out of a hundred a man will shift his eyes just before he draws his gun.

"That was good advice—maybe the best I ever had, maybe not—but I've never been in a gun fight in my life, so I can't really say that it has done me much good.

14

"And I've always remembered the advice that Miss Trimbly, in the fourth or fifth grade, somewhere along in there, gave me. She said, 'If I could just leave one bit of advice with you, Norbert, it would be this: When you get to be a successful, important man—stay humble and unassuming.'

"Beautiful advice, wonderful advice. But I've never become a successful, important man, so I don't need to be humble. I can go right on being a conceited failure—which nobody ever advised me to be.

"It was in 1952, I think, that I had some really great advice. The boss advised me to put everything I had into Consolidated Pumphandle stock. That, as you may recall, was just after the furnace broke down, the house had to be painted, we straightened Sue Jane's teeth, you had your appendix out, and your brother tapped me for that $150. So I couldn't buy Consolidated Pumphandle. It was wonderful advice, though; it made the boss his third million.

"I am loaded with advice which would have deeply affected my life if I had turned out to be a major league baseball manager, a big-game hunter, a novelist, a doctor, an actor, a detective, a salesman, or almost anything else that I'm not."

His wife sighed.

"I suppose," she said, "we'll just have to forget it, then."

"That," he replied, turning once more to the television, "is my advice."

'PERSONAL, BUT NOT TOO'

A television comedy writer and columnist for the Saturday Review, *Goodman Ace is also the author of several books. In this excerpt from his* The Fine Art of Hypochondria, *he discusses his wife's questionable passion for the weather and horoscope columns:*

The two newspaper features widely read in our home are the weather and horoscope columns. Not by me. My wife reads them to me every morning as I leave for the office. I've managed to live with her daily recitals only because of the attendant dialogue, which I will give you a sample of herewith.

"Thundershowers," she says.

"So?" I say, gazing out through a sun-spattered window.

"So, take a raincoat."

I reach into the closet and drag out a raincoat.

"Not that one. I just had it cleaned and pressed.

16

Wear the one I got you for Father's Day."

She did. In 1961. A tissue-paper-thin, shapeless gabardine that even Shylock would not have spat upon. Much less a thundershower.

That night I return carrying the raincoat over my arm.

"What happened to the thundershowers?"

"The wind veered," she says.

"Veered?"

"The wind veered. They announced it on the radio a few minutes after you left. They hadn't expected it to veer but it veered." Veered is the word for the day.

With the horoscope column it becomes a little more complicated. Every morning, after Jane reads my horoscope to me, she also reads me her horoscope for the day. Our horoscopes are seldom compatible and this is a source of great worry to her. She feels certain our marital status is in jeopardy. She has felt this way for about thirty-five years.

It seems I'm a Capricorn. And from the way she has our compatibility figured out she must be a Montague. And you know how they got along. Any day now I expect her to suggest the hemlock bit. One day I suggested that I had never hidden my birth date from her. It was, in fact, her first question after we had been introduced.

17

"I know," she said, "but I thought in time I could overcome it. Being a Libra I'm well balanced."

Actually she's neither. But I don't fight that kind of talk. Being a Capricorn, I never let it get my goat. Instead I try reason, logic, and other unfair tactics, as I do in all our misunderstandings. Most of the time I quietly quote Julius Caesar:

"Men at some time are masters of their fates," I say softly. "The fault, dear Brutus, is not in our stars, but in ourselves, that we are underlings."

"Oh, yeh? And you know what happened to Julius Caesar. Shot down like a dog." Sometimes in the heat of the discussion she corrects herself and says Sid Caesar. . . .

It's when plans are being formulated for traveling South on a winter's vacation that the horoscope gets its biggest play. Certain days are advantageous to think about traveling, certain days to pack for traveling, and finally one certain day actually to travel. For this last step of the trip she adds to the horoscope *The Old Farmer's Almanac*.

Since plane reservations cannot be made horoscopically—and don't think she hasn't phoned to try—she must deduce at least a week in advance a certain propitious trend in her horoscope, which she measures up against the *Farmer's Almanac* for clear flying weather. Somehow she finally manages to match them—you give a little, you take a little—and off we go to the airport.

Once on the plane and we have fastened our seat belts, she is relaxed and content in the indisputable knowledge that her star will see her through. And once the door is banged shut and the engines begin their terrifying din, I notice she supplements it all with a softly murmured prayer. And why not? He did put the stars there, didn't He?

A MAN DOESN'T WANT YOU TO WORRY

Humorous commentaries on marriage and the family are fun reading, especially when written by Jean Kerr, author of The Snake Has All the Lines. *This essay from her book is titled, "The Ten Worst Things About a Man":*

Since a husband supposes, and quite correctly, that you worry a great deal about his health, he will go to any lengths to spare you the least alarm about his physical condition. He will say, as though it were the most casual thing in the world, "Well, I almost keeled over in Grand Central today."

"Good Lord," you will say, "what happened?"

"Nothing, nothing. I leaned against a pillar and I didn't actually fall down."

"But honey, what happened? Did you feel faint? You didn't have a sharp pain in your chest, did you?"

"Oh, no. No, nothing like that."

"Well, what do you mean you almost keeled over?"

"I almost keeled over, that's all."

"But there must have been some *reason*."

"Oh, I guess it's that foot again."

"What foot again? Which foot?"

"Oh, I told you about my foot."

"You most certainly did not tell me anything about your foot."

"The one that's been numb since last summer."

"*Your foot has been numb since last summer?*"

"Now it's more like the whole leg."

"Good heavens, let's call the doctor. Let's call this minute!"

"Why?"

"Why? Are you out of your mind? Because there's something the matter with your leg, that's why!"

"See, there you go, flying off again. I'm sorry I mentioned it, and there's nothing the matter with my leg, nothing."

20

KIDS!

'IS THERE AN ELEPHANT
IN THE HOUSE?'

In her book, The Ziegfelds' Girl, *Patty
Ziegfeld recalls her "abnormally happy
childhood" as the daughter of Florenz Ziegfeld,
the flamboyant producer of the Follies, and
Billie Burke, the actress. In this excerpt, she
tells about the hungry pet elephant
she once owned:*

The baby elephant came next. Daddy had been
down at a Manhattan pier pursuing his favorite
pastime of watching a new shipment of Ringling
animals arrive, and he fell in love with Herman
at first sight. He bought him from John Ringling on the spot, had Joseph Urban design a glass-
jeweled howdah for him, and gave him to me
as a sixth birthday present. Herman was a tre-
mendous sensation at my birthday party, where
he obligingly let all my guests climb on his back
and take rides up and down the driveway.

Herman came complete not only with a howdah, but also with an elephant boy named Henry,
a good-looking lad with wavy black hair and a

22

sallow skin. I fell head over heels in love with him at first sight, partly because of his looks but mostly on account of his calling. The very words "elephant boy" stirred something primitive in my blood—doubtless the same something that made older women swoon over Rudolf Valentino as The Sheik.

I was crazy about Henry, but the baby elephant soon became the most dreadful bore imaginable. He weighed nearly three hundred pounds, so there was no question of being able to romp with him or take him for walks like the dogs. The gardeners loathed him for constantly trampling their plants and flowers. He couldn't be kept in his stall during the day because he lived in constant panic over mice, trumpeting shrilly in alarm if he sighted one scampering over the barn floor.

Worst of all, he never seemed to get enough to eat. He would range the Burkeley Crest grounds like an enormous vacuum cleaner, sucking up any debris in his path. Cigarette butts and Uneeda biscuits were his favorite delicacies but in a pinch he would eat anything. He used to turn up at the kitchen door half a dozen times a day and stick his trunk inside for a handout from Delia, who was far from enchanted at this encroachment of jungle on kitchen.

One morning I was standing in the kitchen doorway eating a Uneeda biscuit when Herman lumbered up and with his trunk, took the biscuit out of my hand and ate it. I stamped my foot at him and went inside for another one. Herman followed me. I suppose it had finally entered his tiny brain that beyond this doorway lay the Great Good Place from whence came all the food.

Delia cringed against the wall screaming and flapping her apron at him, but he merely glanced at her and kept on going, through the kitchen, past the pantry, and up the back stairs, where he got stuck about halfway because the staircase was so narrow. He lifted his trunk and began to trumpet and pound with his hoofs and carry on in a hysterical fashion.

"Who is making all that noise?" Daddy called from the upstairs. "I'm trying to get a little sleep."

"It's Herman, Daddy," I said. "He's stuck."

Daddy appeared at the head of the stairs in his dressing gown.

"You're not supposed to bring Herman into the house," he told me.

"I didn't bring him in," I said. "He just came."

"And why in God's name is he climbing up the stairs?" Daddy asked irritably.

"I think he's hungry," I said.

24

'THE DOCTOR GAME'

Hilda Cole Espy describes the dilemma of a sick mother trying to take care of her four little girls. The episode is taken from her book, Quiet, Yelled Mrs. Rabbit:

One day I was sick. I was feeling terrible. I had a headache. I was nauseous. I had a sore throat. I had chills.

I kept lying down on the living room couch and piteously appealing to my four little girls, "I'm sick. I feel awful. Please be good. Please stay near me because I don't feel strong enough to chase you."

This was plain English, was it not? But they didn't get me or, if they did, they were as ruthless as the Asiatic hordes.

They scampered out of the room, stirred ashes from the fireplace into the sugar bowl, flushed their mittens down the toilet, and drew free form images on the wall paper with liquid-brown shoe polish applicators. They had a happy field day.

I kept hunting them up and crying, as my distraught mother had cried long ago, "What's the matter with you?"

And suddenly I realized, gazing on them with

bilious distaste, that common sense didn't make any sense to them. They didn't know what I *meant* when I said I was feeling bad.

So I was driven to being clever. It's always the last stand for me. I prefer to be honest.

"I know what!" I cried coquettishly, as the four of them were rolling potatoes and onions across the kitchen floor. "Let's pretend I'm sick. Freddy can be the doctor, and Mona can be the nurse, and Joey can be Mrs. Curry [our nearest neighbor] and Cassie can drive the ambulance!"

They jumped up and down and hurled themselves on the linoleum in savage ecstasy of anticipation.

I headed for the living room couch, feeling as if I were wading through waves against an incoming tide. It was better to be down, though; I picked up a pretend telephone and trilled a pretend ring.

"Hello—Mrs. Curry?"

Nearby, Joey picked up a pretend telephone.

"This is Mrs. Curry," she said. "Is this long-distance or what is it, anyway?"

"This is Mrs. Espy. I feel very sick."

"You sound very sick. Did you take any med-sidin?"

"Yes, I did. I took a little bit of everything but it didn't seem to help."

"Well, I will call the doctor and he will give you a shock [shot]."

"All right. Thank you."

"It won't hurt if you be quiet," Mrs. Curry said. "There's no sense of being scared of a shock. Well, goodbye."

She buzzed, making an intense face, like a serious-minded telephone. Freddy picked up her pretend receiver.

"This is the doctor," she reported, brusquely. "I'm at the hospital borning a baby."

"Well, you better hurry up and give Mrs. Espy a shock," Mrs. Curry said, "or she'll get dead."

"I'll call my amberlance," the doctor said.

Soon I had a tinker toy wedged between my teeth for a thermometer, and we kept this thing going until Wede returned from the office. Then I went upstairs, and took two aspirins, and got into bed under a lot of blankets.

A rich man and his daughter are soon parted.

KIN HUBBARD

Many a man who thinks to found a home discovers that he has merely opened a tavern for his friends.

NORMAN DOUGLAS

'WHAT'S IN A NAME?'

Rodello Hunter's book, A House of Many Rooms, *is the chronicle of a rollicking Mormon family in a small Utah town at the turn of the century. The two sketches included here are part of her touching memoir of life in another era:*

Papa christened the twins June and July. Other names had been chosen for them, but Papa capriciously changed his mind on the way up the church aisle. This was not the only time he was to do this. No one knew Tyler was going to be Tyler until he was named that after one of Mama's would-have-been beaus. June didn't mind her name and July put up with hers because, as she always said, she could have been named, and very nearly was, Samantha Maria (pronounced Mair-eye-ee), after Papa's sister. . . .

Aunt Mary used to say: 'When Si and I have children, they are going to call us Father and Mother. Nothing else! There'll be none of this Pa and Ma business in our family.' Well, after a while they had a family grown up enough to talk, and you know what those children called their parents? Mud and Pud."

'FATHER SEWS ON A BUTTON'

Life With Father, *Clarence Day, Jr.'s 1934
classic portrayal of family life was so popular it
became the standard for all memoirs about
fathers. Here Clarence Day describes his father's
trials in sewing on a shirt button:*

Father got holes in his socks even oftener than
we boys did in our stockings. He had long ath-
letic toes, and when he lay stretched out on his
sofa reading and smoking, or absorbed in talking
to anyone, these toes would begin stretching and
wiggling in a curious way by themselves, as though
they were seizing on this chance to live a life of
their own. I often stared in fascination at their
leisurely twistings and turnings, when I should
have been listening to Father's instructions about
far different matters. Soon one and then the other
slipper would fall off, always to Father's surprise,
but without interrupting his talk, and a little later
his busy great toe would peer out at me through
a new hole in his sock. . . .

Buttons were Father's worst trial, however,
from his point of view. Ripped shirts and socks
with holes in them could still be worn, but drawers
with their buttons off couldn't. The speed with
which he dressed seemed to discourage his buttons

30

and make them desert Father's service. Furthermore, they always gave out suddenly and at the wrong moment.

He wanted help and he wanted it promptly at such times, of course. He would appear at Mother's door with a waistcoat in one hand and a disloyal button in the other, demanding that it be sewn on at once. If she said she couldn't just then, Father would get as indignant as though he had been drowning and a lifeguard had informed him he would save him tomorrow.

When his indignation mounted high enough to sweep aside his good judgment, he would say in a stern voice, "Very well, I'll sew it on myself," and demand a needle and thread. This announcement always caused consternation. Mother knew only too well what it meant. She would beg him to leave his waistcoat in her work basket and let her do it next day. Father was inflexible. Moreover, his decision would be strengthened if he happened to glance at her basket and see how many of his socks were dismally waiting there in that crowded exile.

"I've been looking for those blue polka-dotted socks for a month," he said angrily one night before dinner. "Not a thing is done for a man in this house. I even have to sew on my own buttons. Where is your needle and thread?"

Mother reluctantly gave these implements to him. He marched off, sat on the edge of his sofa in the middle of his bedroom, and got ready to work. The gaslight was better by his bureau, but he couldn't sit on a chair when he sewed. It had no extra room on it. He laid his scissors, the spool of thread, and his waistcoat down on the sofa beside him, wet his fingers, held the needle high up and well out in front, and began poking the thread at the eye.

Like every commander, Father expected instant obedience, and he wished to deal with trained troops. The contrariness of the needle and the limp obstinacy of the thread made him swear. He stuck the needle in the sofa while he wet his fingers and stiffened the thread again. When he came to take up his needle, it had disappeared. He felt around everywhere for it. He got up, holding fast to his thread, and turned around, facing the sofa to see where it was hiding. This jerked the spool off onto the floor, where it rolled away and unwound.

The husbands of two of Mother's friends had had fits of apoplexy and died. It frightened her horribly when this seemed about to happen to Father. At the sound of his roars, she rushed in. There he was on the floor, as she had feared. He was trying to get his head under the sofa and he was yelling at something, and his face was such a dark red and his eyes so bloodshot that Mother was terrified. Pleading with him to stop only made him more apoplectic. He said he'd be damned if he'd stop. He stood up presently, tousled but triumphant, the spool in his hand. Mother ran to get a new needle. She threaded it for him and he at last started sewing.

Father sewed on the button in a violent manner, with vicious haulings and jabs. Mother said she couldn't bear to see him—but she couldn't bear to leave the room, either. She stood watching him, hypnotized and appalled, itching to sew it herself, and they talked at each other with vehemence. Then the inevitable accident happened: the needle came forcibly up through the waistcoat, it struck on the button, Father pushed at it harder, and it burst through the hole and stuck Father's finger.

He sprang up with a howl. To be impaled in this way was not only exasperating, it was an affront. He turned to me, as he strode about on the rug, holding onto his finger, and said wrathfully, "It was your mother."

"Why, Clare!" Mother cried.

"Talking every minute," Father shouted at her, "and distracting a man! How the devil can I sew on a button with this gibbering and buzz in my ears? Now see what you made me do!" he added suddenly. "Blood on my good waistcoat! Here! Take the damned thing. Give me a handkerchief to tie up my finger with. Where's the witch-hazel?"

'THE IMPORTANCE OF SPROUTS'

In this book, Give Father a Hard Knock, *Ken Kraft tells what it is like when Father gets caught in the nutritional revolution of his daughter-in-law:*

Father's eyes shifted in a trapped way to the Brussels sprouts. He didn't exactly hate Brussels sprouts, but he would probably have tried stewed grass first if given the choice. He picked up the bowl and started to pass it. "I don't care for—" he said.

"They're to balance your meal, Dad," Pat put in at once. "They're the vitamin C." Father paused, the bowl suspended. "You need C for healthy tissues," she said earnestly. He picked up the serving spoon and found the littlest sprout; he put it on his plate with a martyred air and started to pass the bowl again. "And you need C to build bones," Pat said. Father spooned another sprout onto his plate and thrust the bowl toward me. "Do you know that without vitamin C," Pat said, her eyes wide, "you can get scurvy?" Father desperately ladled out half a dozen more sprouts and passed the bowl at last. I took a few to ward off scurvy and had some wholewheat bread, which she was serving, Pat said, because it was high in phosphorus.

'TAKING THE BITTER WITH THE SWEET'

Mark Twain, in this anecdote from his Autobiography, *recalls his mischievous reputation as a boy—in contrast to the virtuous reputation of his younger brother, Henry—and the problems of justice which arose from this situation:*

Henry never stole sugar. He took it openly from the bowl. Mother knew he wouldn't take sugar when she wasn't looking, but she had her doubts about me. Not exactly doubts, either. She knew very well I *would*. One day when she was not present Henry took sugar from her prized and precious old-English sugar bowl, which was an heirloom in the family—and he managed to break the bowl. It was the first time I had ever had a chance to tell anything on him and I was inexpressibly glad. I told him I was going to tell

on him but he was not disturbed. When my mother came in and saw the bowl lying on the floor in fragments she was speechless for a minute. I allowed that silence to work; I judged it would increase the effect. I was waiting for her to ask, "Who did that?"—so that I could fetch out my news. But it was an error of calculation. When she got through with her silence she didn't ask anything about it—she merely gave me a crack on the skull with her thimble that I felt all the way down to my heels. Then I broke out with my injured innocence, expecting to make her very sorry that she punished the wrong one. I expected her to do something remorseful and pathetic. I told her that I was not the one—it was Henry. But there was no upheaval. She said, without emotion: "It's all right. It isn't any matter. You deserve it for something that you are going to do that I shan't hear about."

There was a stairway outside the house, which led up to the rear part of the second story. One day Henry was sent on an errand and he took a tin bucket along. I knew he would have to ascend those stairs, so I went up and locked the door on the inside and came down into the garden, which had been newly plowed and was rich in choice, firm clods of black mold. I gathered a generous equipment of these and ambushed him.

I waited till he had climbed the stairs and was near the landing and couldn't escape. Then I bombarded him with clods, which he warded off with his tin bucket the best he could, but without much success, for I was a good marksman. The clods smashing against the weather-boarding fetched my mother out to see what was the matter and I tried to explain that I was amusing Henry. Both of them were after me in a minute but I knew the way over that high board fence and escaped for that time. After an hour or two, when I ventured back, there was no one around and I thought the incident was closed. But it was not so. Henry was ambushing me. With an unusually competent aim for him, he landed a stone on the side of my head which raised a bump there which felt like the Matterhorn. I carried it to my mother straightway for sympathy but she was not strongly moved. It seemed to be her idea that incidents like this would eventually reform me if I harvested enough of them.

A mother takes twenty years to make a man of her boy, and another woman makes a fool of him in twenty minutes.

ROBERT FROST

39

'THAT'S NOT ONE OF OURS'

Frank B. Gilbreth, Jr. and Ernestine Gilbreth Carey wrote Cheaper by the Dozen *as a memoir of the childhood they shared with ten brothers and sisters. It was an immediate success as a book and a motion picture. Here they describe their father's attitudes toward his family, Sunday School, and sickness:*

Some people used to say that Dad had so many children he couldn't keep track of them. Dad himself used to tell a story about one time when Mother went off to fill a lecture engagement and left him in charge at home. When Mother returned, she asked him if everything had run smoothly.

"Didn't have any trouble except with that one over there," he replied. "But a spanking brought him into line."

Mother could handle any crisis without losing her composure.

"That's not one of ours, dear," she said. "He belongs next door."

— — —

Dad believed in Sunday school . . . because he thought everyone should have some knowledge of the Bible.

"The successful man knows something about everything," he said.

He used to drive Mother and us to Sunday school, and then sit outside in the car, reading *The New York Times* and ignoring the shocked glares of passing churchgoers.

"You at least might come in where it's warm," Mother told him. "You'll catch your death out here."

"No," Dad replied. "When I go to meet my Maker, I want to be able to tell Him that I did my praying on my own, halted by neither snow nor sleet nor icy stares."

— — —

Dad thought the best way to deal with sickness in the family was simply to ignore it.

"We don't have time for such nonsense," he said.

"There are too many of us. A sick person drags down the performance of the entire group. You children come from sound pioneer stock. You've been given health, and it's your job to keep it. I don't want any excuses. I want you to stay well."

Except for measles and whooping cough, we obeyed orders. Doctors' visits were so infrequent we learned to identify them with Mother's having a baby.

ALL OF US

'THE EXECUTIVE HOUSEWIFE'

The best-laid plans, not only of mice and men, but also of housewives, are apt to go astray, as Patricia Hainline illustrates here in this humorous account of her planned Monday schedule and the unplanned schedule of events:

SUNDAY NIGHT:
Make schedule for coming week.

MONDAY'S SCHEDULE:

7 a.m. Get up; exercise.

7:15   Put clothes in drier. Put clothes in washer.

7:30   Fix face, dress, call family.

7:45   Get breakfast: Pancakes, eggs, juice, bacon, coffee, milk.

8:15   Put second load in washer while family finishes breakfast.

8:45   Send hubby to work. Send children to school.

9:00   Wash dishes. Coffee, newspaper.

43

9:30	Make beds; straighten house.
10:00	Fold clothes, iron.
10:45	Special cleaning (floors today).
11:30	Pick up Carolyn at kindergarten.
11:45	Lunch.
	Afternoon: FREE!

WHAT REALLY HAPPENED:

7 a.m.	Alarm rang. Turned it off.
7:15	Alarm rang. Turned it off.
7:30	Alarm rang. Turned it off.
7:45	Alarm rang. Turned it off.
8:15	Leaped out of bed, hollered at family, put on robe.
8:20	Hollered at family; put cornflakes and milk on table.
8:30	Hollered at family; put juice and toast on table.
9:00	Kids returned—missed bus.
9:05	Dressed. Took kids to school.
9:30	Put clothes in drier. Put clothes in washer.
9:35	Doorbell rang. Gave clothes to man from cleaners.
9:40	Doorbell rang. Told three-year-old Timmy that three-year-old Charlie was in backyard.

9:45	Put dishes in dishwasher.
9:50	Rescued Charlie from Timmy's KO punch.
9:55	Put second load in washer.
10:00	Rescued Timmy from Charlie's KO punch.
10:15	Telephone rang. Kindergarten teacher calling: Carolyn fell; not serious; come and get her.
10:45	Made beds; straightened house.
11:30	Folded clothes.
12:00	Lunch.
12:30	Resolved to do ironing and special cleaning (floors and windows) tomorrow.
	Afternoon: FREE!

The worst misfortune that can happen to an ordinary man is to have an extraordinary father.

AUSTIN O'MALLEY

Families with babies and families without babies are sorry for each other.

EDGAR WATSON HOWE

She treated her hired girl like one of the family —so she quit.   KIN HUBBARD

'I WAS TRAMPLED BY A WHITE ELEPHANT'

Phyllis Diller fans will recognize the comedienne's special brand of humor in this excerpt from Phyllis Diller's Housekeeping Hints:

When buying a new house, you can forget about mortgages, location, and foundations. There are really only three things worthwhile remembering.

1. Buy the biggest house you can find so that when your children are grown up and your husband or some other idiot says, "Why don't you get a job and help out with college expenses?" you can say, "With this house?" Don't bring up the fact that 29 of the 32 rooms are permanently closed off.
2. Buy the house far enough away from school so your kids can't come home for lunch.
3. *Always* buy a house with a fireplace, even if you live in the middle of the desert. Dirt can always be blamed on a faulty flue.

There are two classes of travel—first class, and with children.

ROBERT BENCHLEY

'OF FURLOUGHS AND
FIRST WORDS'

*Only part of the story of the Trapp Family
Singers is portrayed in the popular show,
'The Sound of Music.' Their lives are just
beginning when the musical ends. Here are two
incidents from the family's adventures in
America and Canada, taken from Baroness von
Trapp's book,* The Story of the Trapp
Family Singers:

After a concert in Oklahoma a Colonel came back-
stage, almost moved to tears. With outstretched
arms he congratulated us on the performance.
Born in Hungary, he felt himself a close coun-
tryman to us. He took us all with him, and we
had a lovely evening together. He and Georg
discovered mutual friends and acquaintances, and
when we finally, very, very late, said good-night,
he had become "Uncle Ferdinand." Next day he
came to the train, and just before the last goodbye, he took one of the eagles from his uniform
and pinned it on little Johannes' soldier cap, a
gift from brother Rupert. Half an hour later some
soldiers passed through our car on the way to
the dining car. The first one, especially friendly-
looking, wanting to please that little boy, stepped

47

up before Johannes, saluted, and said:

"Colonel, may I request a furlough?"

Johannes fixed his big blue eyes on the soldier and said:

"Yes, thirty days."

The lucky soldier fished into his pocket and counted out thirty pennies for the gracious little Colonel. I went on reading in my book; then I suddenly discovered there was no Johannes next to me any longer. Alarmed, I got up and looked all over the car, ladies' room, men's room, the next car, and finally found him in the third car, busily selling furloughs all around a crowd of highly amused privates, his little pockets full of pennies. . . .

There were hours and hours of train riding at a time, and you can't tell stories forever, so Johannes had to learn to entertain himself. That day he asked his way through the numbers and letters. Once we stopped for a concert in a convent school somewhere in the Maritime Provinces in northeastern Canada. A darling Reverend Mother occupied herself quite a bit with the little boy, and afterwards she said very pointedly:

"He is a very gifted child, and you should write down everything he says and does. Who knows what will become of him some day! Notice which word he reads first, for instance. Grace sometimes announces itself in such incidents."

A few days later I was holding Johannes on my lap, and we were looking out the window. The train had stopped in a little country town, and our particular car was standing on a street crossing. It was dusk, and the neon signs began to flicker.

Johannes' attention was caught, and slowly and solemnly the promising little child spelled his first word:

"T—A—V—E—R—N."

Before I got married I had six theories about bringing up children; now I have six children, and no theories.

LORD ROCHESTER

COLLECTOR'S ITEMS

Some lives are filled with sorrow and woe
    And some with joys ethereal.
But the days may come and the weeks may go,
    My life is filled with cereal.
My cupboards bulge and my shelves are bunchy
    With morsels crispy or cracked or crunchy,
With rice things, corn things,
    Barley things, wheaten—

All top-of-the-morn things
    And all uneaten.
Ignored they sparkle, unheard they pop
    When once they've yielded the Premium Top.

For Cheerios may be just the fare
    To energize whippersnappers,

But mine consider they've had their share
    As soon as they've filched the wrappers.
Breathes there a child with hopes so dim
    That Kix are innocent Kix to him,
Not loot for filling
    His crowded coffers
With Big New Thrilling
    Premium Offers?
If such (as I fervently doubt) there be,
    He is no kin to my progeny.
As a gardner lusts for a marigold,
    As a miser loves what he mises,
So dotes the heart of a nine-year-old
    On sending away for prizes.
The postman rings and the mail flies hence
With Premium Tops and fifteen cents.
The postman knocks and the gifts roll in:
Guaranteed cardboard, genuine tin,
Paper gadgets and gadgets plastic,
Things that work till you lose the elastic,

Things to molder in drawers and pockets,
Magnets, parachutes, pistols, rockets,
Weapons good for a cop's assistant,
Whistles for dogs that are nonexistent,
Toys designed
    To make mothers tremble,
That fathers find
    They have to assemble,
Things Tom Mixish or Supermanish.
How gadgets come and the box tops vanish!
Then hippity-hop
To the grocer's shop
For a brand-new brand with a Premium Top.

Oh, some lives read like an open book
    And some like a legend hoary.
But life to me, wherever I look,
    Seems one long cereal story.

PHYLLIS MCGINLEY

The house was more covered with mortgages than
with paint.

GEORGE ADE

The greatest thing in family life is to take a hint
when a hint is intended—and not to take a hint
when a hint isn't intended.

ROBERT FROST

'HOW I BECAME THE BOSS
IN MY FAMILY'

*Art Buchwald, the noted columnist, describes
here the unique circumstances and methodology
that enabled him to become 'the boss' of his
family. The selection is from his book,*
How Much Is That In Dollars? :

As I am an American father with an American wife
and three American children, people are constantly amazed to discover that I am the boss in
my family. This I know is a complete switch from
the trend and many people have tried to ascribe
it to the fact that I live in Paris and don't have
the pressure on me that most American males do
in the United States.

But I refuse to believe this is true. I know that
if I lived in the United States I would still be
the boss of the family, and it's not just because I
beat my wife either.

Being the boss in the family is just a state of
mind. . . .

I first became boss of the family about two years
ago and it was quite by accident. Up until then
like all American husbands and fathers I had
been the stereotyped head of the house, the butt
of all the jokes, the good-natured long-suffering

52

male who, because I supplied the bacon, was constantly being put in the frying pan.

And like all American males I didn't seem to mind the role, probably because I didn't know any better.

But then a strange thing happened. I came home one day from the office to discover what is known in France as a Crise de Ménage (a crisis in the house). Everyone from my dear wife to my three little children to the nurse and the cook was up in arms.

It seems the concierge (which in France is a combination of building superintendent, Gestapo agent, and mother-in-law) had insulted the cook and had called her a "name." The cook said she would not work in an apartment house with such a blankety blank and was leaving. My wife was upset and said, "This time the concierge has gone too far and I'm not going to stand for it."

The children all agreed, though they had no idea what anyone was talking about. The nurse said she too was fed up with the concierge and everyone turned to me to see what I was going to do about it, though it was obvious by their expressions they didn't expect much.

My first instinct was to defend the concierge on the grounds that she was old and deaf, and since she was just mean by nature it seemed useless to take offense.

But before I opened my trap I realized this would be useless and all I would receive for my peacemaking efforts was the usual contempt and scorn from my loved ones.

So, much to their surprise, I said, "This is the last straw. No one is going to insult *my* cook and get away with it. I'm going to have it out with her once and for all."

I stormed out of the apartment breathing fire and brimstone and descended to the ground floor where the concierge lived. I found her stirring her witches' broth with a broomstick. She snarled politely, "Oui, Monsieur."

I stared at her and then I put my hand in my pocket and took out twenty francs (four dollars) and I said as I held the francs out, "Why did you insult the cook?"

She took the francs and said, "I didn't mean to insult the cook."

"That's what I told her," I said. "You won't insult her again, will you?"

She put the money into a drawer hastily and replied, "Of course not, Monsieur. Be assured of it."

I stalked upstairs, where the entire family was waiting anxiously for the results.

"Well, I fixed that one," I said triumphantly.

"She'll never insult the cook again."

"What did you say to her?" my wife asked in what seemed for the first time to be a tone of admiration.

"I can't tell you in front of the children," I replied. "But I gave her *more* than a piece of my mind."

The entire family seemed to be thrilled with the results and I could feel a wave of respect sweep through the apartment such as I had never felt before. . . .

'THE KEY TO THE PROBLEM'

Author Giovanni Guareschi has written here about a universal problem: how to distribute keys in a family, and what to do when locked out. The selection is from My Home, Sweet Home, *the English translation of Guareschi's book:*

The first really serious problem that raised its head in our new house was the gate.

The opening and shutting of a small iron gate, painted gray, would not seem in itself to be a complex operation: it was rendered complex by the fact that there was only one key. Anyone without a key had to ring and be let in—and let out.

Even if there had been two or three keys instead of one, of course, they could not have been entrusted to the children. One must never entrust house keys to children.

The problem was extremely serious because Albertino and the Pasionaria [six-year-old Carlotta] went to school at eight in the morning, and to get to school they had to leave the house, and to leave the house they had to use the gate. There was no domestic staff, so it was necessary for father or mother to get up out of bed at eight in the morning to open the gate. And given the case of a father who works at night and goes to bed at about five in the morning, and of a mother who is totally incapable of any kind of activity before 10 A.M., the problem rises to heights unknown.

The first morning I got up. The second morning Margherita got up. The third morning neither of us got up, and Albertino and the Pasionaria, somewhat disgruntled, remained at home.

That evening Margherita and I sat down to consider the situation. . . .

"Margherita," I said, "we are going too far in our search for truth. Truth is usually nearer than that, sometimes indeed within us. The thing is simplicity itself: the children open the gate, they pass through it, close it, giving two turns to the key, then they slip the key into the letter box inside the gate."

Although it was late in the day, we had an immediate dress rehearsal. Albertino and the Pasionaria opened the gate, went out, locked it behind them, and dropped the key into the letter box. Then I took the key of the letter box, opened it, took out the key to the gate, and unlocked the gate. I went out, locked the gate, and dropped the key into the letter box.

"Magnificent!" cried Margherita. "Now I'm going to try it."

Margherita got the key, opened the gate, came out, locked the gate, then slipped the key through the slot of the letter box.

It was now late in the evening, and there we were, all four of us, out in the street. It was cold. I was in my robe and slippers, and so was Margherita. She looked at me perplexed.

"Giovannino, I don't know exactly what's wrong, something is."

"Well, the fact is," I said, "unless the cat opens the letter box, takes out the key to the gate and lets us in, we'll have to spend the night in the street. Moreover, we're going to be in exactly the same situation tomorrow morning."

When I mentioned a gate, did you think of the everyday kind, iron latticework put together more or less for art's sake? That's precisely the kind of gate we had. But my farsightedness had added a strong, thick wire netting to prevent ill-intentioned people from putting a hand through the bars to get at the lock or the letter box.

We persuaded Albertino to climb the wall, and as he was doing it, an elderly couple passing by observed loudly that only in this day and age do parents have the moral laxity to teach such tricks to their children.

"In my day," said the man, "fathers spanked children who tried to climb over walls and gates."

"And mothers," said the woman, "didn't parade through the streets at night in their robes."

With Albertino on the other side of the wall, there should have been no problem. Of course the letter box was locked. Margherita, after she had taken the gate key from the letter box, had closed and locked the box and put that key in her pocket. All she had to do now was pass the key to Albertino. Here, however, Margherita was guilty of a degree of thoughtlessness: she passed the key through—and dropped it in the slot of the letter box.

Even after I climbed over the wall, at no small sacrifice to my person, the incident was not yet

closed: after me came Margherita, whose good fortune it was to have me to support her morally on one side of the wall and physically on the other. After she touched ground, there was the Pasionaria's voice from the street: "And me, who's going to get me over?"

So I made the dangerous journey again: back to the street, hand the Pasionaria over the wall to Margherita, climb over and down again. Three round trips in all.

Back in the house, we faced the problem of recovering the two keys. Margherita lightly suggested that we break the lock on the gate. It seemed simpler to me to unscrew the letter box and break the gate open. And so we did, and at midnight, order had been restored.

*Set in Caslon Old Style, a roman based on the designs
of the 18th century English typefounder William Caslon.
Printed on Hallmark Eggshell Book paper.
Designed by Claudia Becker.*